Claude
Monet

By Steven Z. Levine

RIZZOLI ART SERIES
Series Editor: Norma Broude

Claude
Monet

(1840–1926)

MONET sounds like the French word for coin (*monnaie*), and today from Japan to Germany to Johannesburg Monet spells money—big money. His paintings sell in the high six and seven figures. His house and gardens at Giverny annually generate millions of dollars for French tourism as well as for the luxury trade in Giverny-inspired implements for table, bed, and bath. Garden catalogs promise the perennial perfection of Monet's rainbow-hued calendar of flowers. And blockbuster exhibitions of his work feature shops replete with audioguides, videotapes, reproductions, clothing, stationery, and books: blank books, cookbooks, garden books, children's books, postcard books, photography books, art books (just like this one, perhaps).

Why the pervasive and persistent Monetmania? A recently influential formula by the art historian T. J. Clark proposes that the popularity of the art of Monet and his Impressionist colleagues can best be understood in reference to its "complaisance at modernity."[1] This is to say that in seeming to turn his back on the alienating effects of industrialization and class division in capitalist society, Monet escaped into a harmonious world of timeless, natural beauty to which we still long to escape, though with ever greater disingenuous denial of the contentious conditions of our cutthroat public sphere. Within the social history of art an alternative approach to this condemnation of the escapist allure of Monet's art is made by those who justify Monet's appeal by insisting that the painter's cultivation of his art at Giverny entailed for him, and can entail for us, an implicit critique of the corruption and commodification of consumer society. This argument was first made a century ago in the name of political anarchism and artistic individualism, when Monet's posture of personal autonomy in the artistic sphere was seen as a radical rebuke of the French Republican state, which for many citizens seemed to pay only lip service to its own revolutionary ideals of freedom. Accordingly, in the words of Monet's friend Stéphane Mallarmé, at a time when the artist "is on strike against society," the true painter or poet is "a man who isolates himself in order to sculpture his own tomb."[2] Monet's career-long enterprise of self-reflection may thus be seen to manifest a modern version of the Narcissus myth.[3]

As traditionally represented by poets and painters such as Ovid or Poussin (fig. 1), Narcissus rejects the repeated appeals for social and sexual intercourse of the nymph Echo to scrutinize instead the beautiful image of himself he finds reflected in the water; in the ensuing process of coming to the paradoxical recognition that the image is his own and yet cannot be possessed, Narcissus is transformed into the flower that bears his name, and he dies. Western culture has been divided for two thousand years over what Narcissus's destiny represents: either lethal self-infatuation or lucid self-abnegation, either the irresponsible fixation upon fleeting appearances at the expense of productive relations with others or the thoughtful interrogation of the corporeal and corporate constraints upon our precariously instituted self-consciousness. Monet's advocates and antagonists have been arguing both sides of this complex debate for more than a century now—in effect a debate between the rival viewpoints of Marx and Freud—and it is no surprise that we are no closer to consensus than ever. Indeed some will see in the watery reflections of Monet's art the merest enthrallment by the surface phenomenon of vision, whereas others will regard those same surfaces of water, sky, and paint as moving, mute acknowledgments of the mortal condition we all, for a time, share. As Paul Valéry, another of Monet's poet friends, wrote of Narcissus, "Is it not at all to think of death to regard oneself in the mirror? Does one not see there one's perishable part? The immortal sees there the mortal. A mirror takes us out of our skin, of our face. Nothing resists one's double."[4]

Monet's first preserved painting (plate 1) depicts not the youth of myth but his rural nineteenth-century counterpart, a young fisherman seated in solitary contemplation by the

1. Nicolas Poussin. *Echo and Narcissus.* c. 1630. Oil on canvas, 29¼ x 39¼". Musée du Louvre, Paris. Photograph courtesy Réunion des Musées Nationaux

mirrored banks of a Norman pool or stream. Slender poplars are inverted in the water in this painting, which is seemingly free of all allegorical intention and yet, as Théophile Thoré, one of the period's principal critics, had earlier asserted, even "the most spontaneous painters, devoted solely to the image without any preoccupation for the underlying thought, sometimes make pictures in which reflection may discover symbolic poems and analogies unsuspected by the author."[5] What then might these unsuspected analogies and symbols be?

Monet made his painting of a modern, field-and-stream Narcissus in 1858 under the auspices of Eugène Boudin (1824–1898), a landscape and seascape painter from Monet's hometown of Le Havre who served as the eighteen-year-old painter's first mentor. The very different examples of the provincial and Parisian realism of Gustave Courbet

2. Edouard Manet. *Claude and Camille Monet in the Studio-Boat.* 1874. Oil on canvas, 31½ x 38½". Bayerische Staatsgemäldesammlungen, Munich. Photograph courtesy Artothek

(1819–1877) and Edouard Manet (1832–1883) would subsequently have still greater impact on the formation of Monet's pictorial enterprise, but for the moment it was the rustic Romanticism of Boudin that placed its seal on Monet's artistic absorption in nature. Triumphant in France from the time of Jean-Jacques Rousseau one hundred years earlier,[6] this solitary scrutiny of nature as the source and mirror of the artist's own consciousness of self was carried forward to the generation of Boudin and Monet by the meditative images and on-site sketching practices of landscape painters such as Camille Corot (1796–1875), Théodore Rousseau (1812–1867), and Charles-François Daubigny (1817–1878). It is their introspective voices we hear in Monet's repeated insistence on the necessary solitude of the artist, sentiments he anxiously articulated from the beginning of his career to the end:

> It would be better to be all alone, and yet, all alone there are a lot of things that one cannot make out. [15 July 1864]
>
> Don't you think that precisely with nature alone one does better? . . . What I will do here will at least have the merit of resembling no one, at least I think so, because it will simply be the expression of what I will have felt, me personally. [December 1868]
>
> I am enchanted to be alone, it seems to me that I am going to work better even in bad weather, for alone I cannot stay unoccupied. [1 November 1885]
>
> I have too great a need to be alone and tranquil. [21 January 1888]
>
> I have returned to isolate myself here and to try to take up again the taste for work in this place where I made so many things fifteen years ago. [28 February 1896]
>
> I wish to devote the time remaining to me to live to work, uniquely in order to do better if my sight permits. For this, I wish to live in solitude and peace of mind. [3 January 1920][7]

The artistic cultivation of solitude was controversial at the beginning of Monet's career, and it has remained so. In 1860 the poet and critic Charles Baudelaire pointed to the use of drugs as a dangerous instance of self-absorption, which "like all solitary joys, renders the individual useless to others and society superfluous for the individual, pushing

him ceaselessly to admire himself and precipitating him day by day toward the luminous gulf where he admires his face of Narcissus."[8] So we may well ask just what sort of useless, solitary joy Monet is up to in his landscape of a reflecting pool in Normandy in 1858, or in a larger painting made a decade later at Bennecourt, midway along the Seine between Rouen and Paris, where his mistress and new baby son's mother, Camille Doncieux, is seen absorbed in the contemplation of the river's reflection, the view from behind inviting us to share in her private vision even as we remain detached voyeurs (plate 2).

By the time Monet made this painting in 1868 he had already experienced both success and failure at the annual art exhibitions of the French state known as the Salon. At the Salon of 1865 a pair of rather large, conventional seascapes were praised for Monet's "bold manner of seeing things and of imposing himself upon the attention of the spectator."[9] He attained further critical success when he exhibited a life-size portrait of his mistress at the Salon of 1866, but during the course of the next four years the Salon jury rejected seven of the eight large-scale pictures he submitted, including *Women in the Garden* (1867) and *The Luncheon* (1868). Isolated from the public by these official acts of exclusion, Monet turned to the increasingly prominent private dealers, such as Paul Durand-Ruel, whose galleries provided an alternative market for Monet's inexpensive, small-scale, brightly colored, and vigorously brushed open-air landscapes, which at that time were highly controversial yet form the basis of Monet's reputation today. Monet also sought public endorsement of his work in the series of independent exhibitions he organized along with his colleagues Cézanne, Degas, Morisot, Pissarro, Renoir, and Sisley, starting in 1874. Known at first as the *Société anonyme des artistes peintres,* this group of artists soon came to be known as the Impressionists, largely on the basis of the title of Monet's painting of the foggy port at Le Havre, *Impression, Sunrise* (plate 3), a work that was singled out by the critics for both ridicule and praise.[10]

The word "impression" had been a familiar term of Salon criticism for many years, but its accepted reference to a painter's allegedly objective representation of the striking visual effects associated with natural phenomena such as sunrise or fog soon gave way to the notion of an illegitimate eccentricity of depiction born of technical incompetence and subjective caprice. Thus *Impression, Sunrise* seemed to one hostile critic as though "treated by the infantile hand of a schoolboy who spreads out colors for the first time on any old surface," and yet to a more sympathetic reviewer it "rings out with the accents of the morning gun."[11] For the first critic, who focused on formal considerations alone, Monet's loose, emphatic brushwork was fundamentally illegible in terms of the conventional norms of drawing and perspective. For the second critic, however, who addressed the painting both as a record of nature and as a personal expression by the artist, the brushwork of Monet and his colleagues conjured up vivid associations: "They are *impressionists* in the sense that they render not the landscape, but the sensation produced by the landscape." In spite of this useful formula, the critic, Jules-Antoine Castagnary, worried that in single-mindedly pursuing their own sensations the Impressionists might leave nature entirely behind: "From idealization to idealization, they will wind up at this degree of romanticism without brake where nature is no more than a pretext for reverie, and where the imagination becomes impotent to formulate anything other than personal, subjective fantasies, without echo in general reason, because they are without control and any possible verification in reality."[12] Not long after the Impressionists ceased to exhibit as a group in 1886 Castagnary's fear of artistic subjectivity came to be realized in the transvalued form of Mallarmé's famous definition of art: "*To name* an object is to suppress three-quarters of the pleasure of the poem that is made to be guessed at bit by bit; *to suggest* it, there is the dream."[13]

Mallarmé's dreamlike poetry was adduced in 1891 as a paradigm of Monet's suggestive art by their mutual friend, the novelist and critic Octave Mirbeau. With him we do well to wonder what dream—and whose dream other than our own—Monet's paintings suggest. We might imagine that the dream in question is that of the Narcissus-like fisherman of 1858 or his female counterpart of 1868 or, alternatively, of Monet as he projects himself into their roles or looks down from his window at the fog-bound port of Le Havre at the rising sun reflected in the water. Mallarmé translated a popular book of mythology in which this reflective motif of the sun and the sea is seen as a natural equivalent of the Narcissus myth. I make no such explicit claim for any of Monet's paintings of the sun reflected in water, but I do wish to present *The Studio-Boat* of 1874 (plate 4), in whose interior the artist's shadowy presence is perhaps dimly visible, as an emblematic dramatization of Monet's modern enterprise of self-reflection.[14] Derived from a craft used by Daubigny to paint the rivers of France, Monet's floating studio was moored during the 1870s at Argenteuil in the outer suburbs of Paris, and it was there in 1874 that the quintessential Parisian painter Manet painted his friend Monet in the rapt self-absorption of work (fig. 2).

Seated by Monet's side in Manet's painting is Camille Monet, the painter's wife since 1870, now cast in the subordinate role of Echo, a necessary support for his domestic well-being but not a sufficient object for his artistic gaze. In the years to come Monet increasingly turned away from the human figure to focus on the reflective properties of the landscape, as we see in *The Pond at Montgeron* of 1876 (plate 5), where two-thirds of the surface of this large, still painting is filled to the brim with the watery repetition of the surrounding scene. Even here, however, a second glance will show Alice Hoschedé—the wealthy owner of the estate, the painter's patron at this time, and later his mistress and second wife—standing with her rod at the ready in silent contemplation of her inverted image on the surface of the water as her children take up secondary positions along the banks. A similar scene of suspended animation makes solitary Narcissuses of seven men fishing on the Seine (plate 6), each of them alone in their joint anonymity in this plunging view from Poissy where Monet briefly lived in 1882 at a time of general financial crisis in France as well as personal turmoil after the death of his wife.

A less alienated sense of shared contemplation seems to characterize a large painting of 1887, *In the Norwegian Canoe* (plate 7), in which Monet depicted Mme Hoschedé's daughters, Germaine, Suzanne, and Blanche (ages 14, 19, and 22), fishing, floating, and gazing into the water's dark depths. Painted eight years after the death of Camille Monet

and four years after Monet and Mme Hoschedé set up joint housekeeping at Giverny, the painting recapitulates the cultural stereotype of feminine introspection that Monet had addressed in *On the Seine at Bennecourt* and *The Pond at Montgeron* and that corresponds to the initial identification by Narcissus of his image as that of the nymph of the spring (or, in another version of the myth, as that of his dead twin sister). Monet frequently employed Suzanne Hoschedé to repeat the poses formerly enacted by his late wife, and several times he depicted Blanche Hoschedé at work at her painter's easel amid the fields and waters of Giverny. A number of these feminine, familial scenes, including *In the*

3. Monet's photograph of his own shadow in the water-lily pool. c. 1903–1907. Collection Philippe Piguet

Norwegian Canoe, were featured in a special grouping of "essays in open-air figures" at a major retrospective exhibition in 1889 that saw the widespread consolidation of Monet's critical reputation.[15] These paintings of women in nature tell a repeated tale of longing and loss even as they retrieve the lapsed ambitions of the Salon paintings of the 1860s, ambitions to depict modern life on a monumental scale that may have been reactivated at this time by the notoriety of a painting such as *A Sunday Afternoon on La Grande Jatte* (1884–1886) by Monet's younger, Neo-Impressionist rival, Georges Seurat (1859–1891).

As it turned out, however, the large-scale figurative paintings of 1889 were already an anachronism in Monet's art. By 1891, when Monet painted *The Four Trees* (plate 8) as but one canvas in his fifteen-part series of paintings of poplars, monumentality was achieved as an aggregate effect of the entire installation. Here the mythological drama of a Narcissus-like gazer was transformed into the vicissitudes of Monet's self-mirroring tree "of allegorical profile."[16] "The world is an immense Narcissus in the process of thinking itself"—these words were written in 1892 by Joachim Gasquet, a symbolist writer known to art historians as a biographer of Cézanne, who insisted that the Impressionist painting hitherto understood as merely representing a particular natural effect was nothing of the kind: "The landscape reflects itself, humanizes itself, thinks itself in me. . . . I would be the subjective consciousness of this landscape, as my canvas would be its objective consciousness."[17] Or as Monet said of his *Poplars*, "I have yet again struggled with the admirable landscape motif that I had to do in all weathers in order to make only one which would not be of any weather, any season" (November 1891).[18] An admiring critic called the *Poplars* Monet's "idea-tree."[19]

As early as 1880 Monet's friend Théodore Duret insisted on the subjective dimension of Monet's recursive practice of painting in series. The convention of the Salon was to make single, large, self-sufficient tableaux, but for reasons that were not only commercial Monet made series of small, fragmentary but mutually related pictures instead: "In spite of the repetitive absorption in landscape motifs, no artist has less known monotony for, working in front of nature, in ultimate contact with her, he seizes all her mobile aspects and thus can perpetually renew himself."[20] Duret's portrayal of the dramatic encounter between the male artist and female nature manifests a deep metaphor of nineteenth-century European culture, as Norma Broude has shown,[21] and indeed my stress here is on the notion of the series as an ongoing process of self-transformation through which Monet expressed his desires and fears as an embodied, gendered being. As Mirbeau wrote of his friend in 1889, "one feels rumbling in him the impatience of fecundity, moving in him the ferocious and masculine desire to embrace everything, to grasp everything, to submit everything to the domination of his genius."[22]

The language of genius, domination, and masculine desire may seem offensive to us today,[23] but it was representative of the late nineteenth-century cult of the self of which Mirbeau was an important proponent and from which the achievements and excesses of our own so-called culture of narcissism have directly evolved.[24] Monet's anarchistic self-affirmation in art was widely seen as a politically exemplary repudiation of the conformist productions of the popular Salon painters of the day—in his work "all contemplate what they could be and take consciousness of themselves"[25]—and yet in his letters Monet repeatedly stressed his difficulty in "recognizing himself" in his work:

> *The farther I go, the more I seek the impossible, the unseizable, and at moments I fear losing myself in it. [25 February 1888]*
>
> *The farther I go, the more I seek the impossible and the more I feel powerless. [10 March 1888]*
>
> *I thought that I was going to do astounding things, but alas, the farther I go, the more difficulty I have in rendering what I would like. [8 April 1889]*
>
> *I have taken up things impossible to do: water with grass that undulates in the depths, it is admirable to see, but it is enough to drive one mad to wish to do it. [22 June 1890]*
>
> *I add and I lose certain things. In sum, I am seeking the impossible. [9 April 1892]*
>
> *Alas! I can only repeat this, that the farther I go, the more trouble I have in rendering what I feel, and I say that anyone who claims to have finished a canvas is terribly proud; to finish meaning complete, perfect. I work by force, without advancing. [28 March 1893][26]*

The last two letters quoted here were written from Rouen, where Monet spent two successive winter campaigns obsessively painting, scraping, and repainting his *Cathedrals* (see plate 9), twenty of which were eventually exhibited at the galleries of Durand-Ruel in 1895.

Described by Gustave Geffroy, Monet's future biographer, as the painter's "dream of light which he causes to rise up before him in the stones of Rouen," the *Cathedrals* were commonly understood as Monet's subjective transpositions of the changing circumstances of light and weather that may once have briefly prevailed in the outside world: "The real is present, and it is transfigured. . . . It is everywhere a reality at once immutable and changing. Matter is present, submitted to a luminous phantasmagoria. What Monet paints is the space that exists between himself and things."[27] The precarious traversability of that intermediate space is registered, perhaps, in the roughly encrusted painted surfaces of Monet's stoneless facades; yet its unbridgeable abyss may also be acknowledged in the tiny gazing figures who are overwhelmingly dwarfed by the cathedral's stone mass.

Painted from shop windows in Rouen and repainted in the studio at Giverny, the *Cathedrals* represented a departure from Monet's standard practice of open-air landscape painting, and their special serial demands seem to have exhausted him: "I have just spent almost a week lazing about, looking at the water, the flowers, the sky" (24 May 1895).[28] An early result of this aquatic reverie was the eighteen-part series of *Mornings on the Seine* (see plate 10), exhibited in 1898. One critic anxiously objected that "nature reflects herself in him rather more than he reflects her," but another insisted that though "man is no more visible here, . . . the personality of the painter, it is."[29] Do Monet's paintings passively reflect a pregiven, feminine, and hence awesome nature; do they actively display the masculine consciousness of self-reflection; or do they do—and undo—both? Critics then and now have seen in the reflective symmetries and fractured surfaces of Monet's paintings what they have desired or feared to see there. As one of them remarked, "nothing exists of which we have not projected the objective vision from out of ourselves."[30]

By the end of the 1890s Monet's paintings were selling at high prices at home and abroad, especially to Americans in the social circle of the artist's Impressionist colleague, Mary Cassatt (1844–1926). Monet's formerly spurned works were now deemed highly desirable, and with the proceeds of his sales he was able to transform his property at Giverny into the work of environmental art that dazzled early visitors and commentators such as Mallarmé, Valéry, and Marcel Proust. An old Norman orchard became Monet's famous flower garden, and the still more famous water garden (plates 11, 13, 14) took shape on an adjacent piece of land directly across a narrow communal road and a tiny spur rail-

4. Monet painting by the water-lily pool, 8 July 1915.
Collection Philippe Piguet

5. Monet, Germaine Hoschedé-Salerou, and Blanche Hoschedé-Monet in his third studio with self-portrait (now destroyed). c. 1917. Collection Philippe Piguet

way line. Critics in the Marxist tradition have made much of Monet's artistic erasure of the railway (which in the 1870s he had depicted in Paris at the Gare Saint-Lazare) as a sign of his regressive withdrawal from the painting of reality in all its messy contradictions of property and class.[31] This is to assume, erroneously I believe, that a painter *re*-presents some preexistent set of perceptual or social facts from a single, fixed perspective. My reading of Monet's series is offered instead on behalf of the notion of a continuous metamorphosis of the painter's self by way of an ongoing pictorial engagement with nature. This dialectical and interminable enterprise of self-reflection provides, in my view, a thoroughly urgent occasion for the labor that is art.

"Superbly isolated, a man apart, an exceptional nature,"[32] Monet repeatedly bent over the surface of his water-lily pool and, like Narcissus, eventually recognized himself there:

> *I have undertaken not a few new things that I could not do, especially on account of this impossible weather. [21 May 1898]*
> *In sum, I am not letting go and am beginning a bit to refind myself. [5 July 1899]*
> *I am working but with quite a lot of difficulty in spite of the fine weather, but more and more I have difficulty in satisfying myself. [13 June 1906]*
> *These landscapes of water and reflections have become an obsession. It is beyond my powers as an old man, and yet I want to arrive at rendering what I feel. I have destroyed some. . . . Some I recommence. [11 August 1908][33]*

Monet eventually exhibited forty-eight of these much-maligned and mutilated *Water Lilies* at Durand-Ruel's in 1909. The figureless canvas illustrated here (plate 11) can be seen to reincarnate the ghostly waterside gaze of Camille Doncieux from forty years before (plate 2), with the enframing foliage of 1868 now transformed into that of the funereal weeping willow, recently evoked by Monet's poet friend Maurice Rollinat: "The Narcissus of the vegetable realm / Still admires in the water / Its green face that weeps."[34] In a photograph presumably taken by Monet himself around the date of this painting we see his own Narcissus-like shadow captured on the water at his feet (fig. 3), and indeed it was this unprecedentedly "egoistic" subordination of the spectator to the artist's personal viewpoint that proved to be

tremendously disorienting to the critics at the exhibition of 1909: "There is here an affirmation of authority and independence, a supremacy of the I, which offends our vanity and humiliates our pride."[35] Just what is at stake in this simultaneous affirmation and denunciation of Monet's eye/I?

"Never has a painter more resolutely denied matter. . . . The touch imitates nothing, it evokes. . . . I would not affirm that he is truly convinced that nature exists."[36] Whether it is the neo-Gothic architecture of the Houses of Parliament in London (plate 12) or an unpeopled corner of the pond at Giverny (plate 13), Monet's work is increasingly seen by the critics as the means by which the painter achieves "consciousness of himself."[37] In interviews of the period Monet seems to debunk the modern discourse of the self in which his art had become notably caught up, preferring instead to relate his work to the old masters: "They considered themselves like artisans, good workers always in school. One had not yet invented the mission of art, the sacerdotalism of genius, an omniscient individualism and other nonsense."[38] Monet (if indeed these are his words or sentiments) was quite right to insist on the notion of the autonomous individual as a historically recent social construction of debatable and even dubious utility, yet ironically it was precisely around his art that this key idea of modern culture came to be massively and systematically deployed (fig. 4).[39]

With respect to this notional self, however, the Nietzschean fullness of self of about 1889 soon came to be voided in the somber aftermath of World War I. "I am seeking the impossible," Monet wrote to Geffroy (10 September 1918), and in the face of the final *Water Lilies* (plate 14), which are at once a monumental womb and tomb, Geffroy claimed to recognize "the annihilation of [Monet's] individuality in the eternal nirvana of things."[40] This Buddhist idiom of selflessness brings the understanding of Monet's art very close to Freud's contemporaneous notion of a repetitive urgency "beyond the pleasure principle" that drives us toward the dissolution of our material being in the preemptive contemplation of our own death.[41] This mortal acknowledgment of the full self as a false lure, an illusory projection, a fragmentary reflection radically cut off from the flux of material embodiment is illustrated for me in Monet's lone surviving self-portrait from his final decade (plate 15).[42] In a photograph from about 1917 (fig. 5) of Monet in his wartime studio standing in front of a life-size mirror of Narcissus, surrounded by panels of *Water Lilies* to be given as a memorial of victory to France and accompanied by two of his Hoschedé stepdaughters who remained faithful Echos to the end, we see the subsequently destroyed mate of Monet's aqueous self-portrait as though floating on the surface of the water-lily pool. At once the loyal realist of the generation of Courbet, Manet, and Baudelaire as well as the reluctant symbolist of the circle of Mallarmé and Valéry, Monet could embody himself as Narcissus in the panoramic field of his *Water Lilies* only through this impermanent staging of an unpaintable myth. But we are free to see in the pictorial play between the immaterial disembodiment of his gaze and the palpable repetition of his touch the relentless temporal rhythms of the myth, "the secret of oblivion in which our meager individualities lose themselves."[42] Perhaps in Monet's *Water Lilies* "presentness is grace"; and then again, sadly, perhaps not.[43] It all depends on how we mirror ourselves in his reflective art before the gaze goes blank.

For Susan and Madeleine

NOTES

1. T. J. Clark, *The Painting of Modern Life: Paris in the Art of Manet and His Followers* (New York: Alfred A. Knopf, 1985), p. 268.
2. Stéphane Mallarmé, *Oeuvres complètes* (Paris: Gallimard, 1945), pp. 869–870.
3. Steven Z. Levine, *Monet, Narcissus, and Self-Reflection: The Modernist Myth of the Self* (Chicago: University of Chicago Press, 1994).
4. Paul Valéry, *Oeuvres* (Paris: Gallimard, 1957), Vol. I, p. 332.
5. Théophile Thoré, *Salons de T. Thoré 1844, 1845, 1846, 1847, 1848* (Paris: Librairie Internationale, 1868), p. 105.
6. Charles Taylor, *Sources of the Self: The Making of the Modern Identity* (Cambridge, Mass.: Harvard University Press, 1989).
7. Daniel Wildenstein, *Claude Monet: Biographie et catalogue raisonné* (Lausanne and Paris: La Bibliothèque des Arts and Wildenstein Institute, 1975–1991), Vol. I, letters nos. 8, 44; Vol. II, no. 605; Vol. III, no. 812; Vol. V, nos. 1327, 3050 (2329b).
8. Charles Baudelaire, *Oeuvres complètes* (Paris: Gallimard, 1975),Vol. I, p. 440.
9. Paul Mantz, "Salon de 1865," *Gazette des Beaux-Arts*, 1st ser. 19 (July 1865), p. 26.
10. Richard Shiff, "The End of Impressionism," and Paul Tucker, "The First Exhibition in Context," in Charles S. Moffett, *The New Painting: Impressionism 1874–1886* (San Francisco: The Fine Arts Museums of San Francisco, 1986), pp. 61–89, 93–117.
11. Marc de Montifaud [Marie-Amélie Chartroule de Montifaud], "Exposition du boulevard des Capucines," *L'Artiste* (1 May 1874), pp. 308–309; and Jules-Antoine Castagnary, "L'Exposition du boulevard des Capucines: Les Impressionnistes," *Le Siècle* (29 April 1874).
12. Castagnary, 1874.
13. Mallarmé, *Oeuvres complètes*, p. 869.
14. Paul Hayes Tucker, *Monet at Argenteuil* (New Haven: Yale University Press, 1982), p. 112.
15. *Claude Monet–Auguste Rodin: Centenaire de l'exposition de 1889* (Paris: Musée Rodin, 1989).
16. Louis Désiré, "Claude Monet," *L'Evénement* (19 May 1891).
17. Joachim Gasquet, *Narcisse* (Paris: Librairie de France, 1931), p. 45, and idem, *Cézanne* (Paris: Bernheim-Jeune, 1921), in *Conversations avec Cézanne*, ed. P. M. Doran (Paris: Macula, 1978), p. 110.
18. Wildenstein, Vol. III, letter no. 1124.
19. Clément Janin, "Claude Monet," *L'Estafette* (10 March 1892).
20. Théodore Duret, *Critique d'avant-garde* (Paris: G. Charpentier, 1885), pp. 103–104.
21. Norma Broude, *Impressionism, A Feminist Reading: The Gendering of Art, Science, and Nature in the Nineteenth Century* (New York: Rizzoli, 1991). Broude's attentive reading of my manuscript helped clarify a number of points in the presentation here.
22. Octave Mirbeau, "Claude Monet," in *Exposition Claude Monet–Auguste Rodin: Galerie Georges Petit* (Paris: Imprimerie de l'Art, 1889), p. 19.
23. Griselda Pollock, *Vision and Difference: Femininity, Feminism, and Histories of Art* (London: Routledge, 1988), and Tamar Garb, "Gender and Representation," in Francis Frascina, Nigel Blake, Briony Fer, Tamar Garb, and Charles Harrison, *Modernity and Modernism: French Painting in the Nineteenth Century* (New Haven: Yale University Press and Open University, 1993), pp. 219–290.
24. Christopher Lasch, *The Culture of Narcissism: American Life in an Age of Diminishing Expectations* (New York: W. W. Norton, 1979).
25. Camille Mauclair [Séverin Faust], "Notes sur l'idée pure," *Mercure de France*, n.s. 6 (September 1892), p. 45.
26. Wildenstein, Vol. III, letters nos. 854, 943, 1151, 1201; Vol. V, nos. 1060, 2732 (842a).
27. Gustave Geffroy, "Claude Monet," *Le Journal* (10 May 1895).
28. Wildenstein, Vol. V, letter no. 2938 (1300b).
29. Gabriel Séailles, "L'Impressionnisme," in *L'Almanach du bibliophile pour l'année 1898* (Paris: E. Pellatan, 1898), p. 47, and Charles Saunier, "Claude Monet," *La Revue Blanche* 23 (15 December 1900), p. 624.
30. André Fontainas, in *Anthologie des poètes français contemporains: Le Parnasse et les écoles postérieures au Parnasse* (Paris: C. Delagrave, [1906]), Vol. II, p. 521.
31. See the contrasting approaches to this issue in Nigel Blake and Francis Frascina, "Modern Practices of Art and Modernity," and Charles Harrison, "Impressionism, Modernism and Originality," in *Modernity and Modernism*, pp. 125–138, 214–217.
32. Arsène Alexandre, "Un Paysagiste d'aujourd'hui et un portraitiste de jadis," *Comoedia* (8 May 1909).
33. Wildenstein, Vol. III, letter no. 1407 bis; Vol. IV, nos. 1468, 1805, 1854.
34. Maurice Rollinat, *Paysages et paysans: Poésies* (Paris: G. Charpentier, 1899), p. 37.
35. Roger Marx, "Les 'Nymphéas' de M. Claude Monet," *Gazette des Beaux-Arts*, 4th ser. 1 (June 1909), p. 523.
36. Louis Gillet, "L'Epilogue de l'impressionnisme: Les 'Nymphéas' de M. Claude Monet," *Revue Hebdomadaire* 8 (21 August 1909), pp. 402–403.
37. Thiébault-Sisson, "Claude Monet," *Le Temps* (6 April 1920).
38. Marc Elder, *A Giverny, chez Claude Monet* (Paris: Bernheim-Jeune, 1924), pp. 53–54.
39. Robert C. Solomon, *Continental Philosophy since 1750: The Rise and Fall of the Self* (Oxford: Oxford University Press, 1988).
40. Wildenstein, Vol. IV, letter no. 2281; and Gustave Geffroy, *Claude Monet: Sa vie, son oeuvre* (Paris: G. Crès, 1922), p. 335.
41. Steven Z. Levine, "Monet, Fantasy, and Freud," in *Psychoanalytic Perspectives on Art*, ed. Mary Mathews Gedo (Hillsdale, N.J.: Analytic Press, 1985), Vol. I, pp. 29–55.
42. Jacques Lacan, "The Mirror Stage as Formative of the Function of the I," in *Ecrits: A Selection*, trans. Alan Sheridan (New York: W. W. Norton, 1977), pp. 1–7.
43. Michael Fried, "Art and Objecthood," in *Minimal Art: A Critical Anthology*, ed. Gregory Battcock (New York: E. P. Dutton, 1968), p. 147. The tensions in this essay between the constitution of the self and its critical deconstruction rehearse the terms of the twenty-five-year debt I owe to the writing and teaching of Michael Fried.

FURTHER READING

Gordon, Robert, and Andrew Forge. *Monet*. New York: Harry N. Abrams, 1983.

Herbert, Robert. "Method and Meaning in Monet." *Art in America* 67 (September 1979), pp. 90–108.

House, John. *Monet: Nature into Art*. New Haven: Yale University Press, 1986.

Isaacson, Joel. *Claude Monet: Observation and Reflection*. Oxford: Phaidon, 1978.

Joyes, Claire. *Claude Monet: Life at Giverny*. New York and Paris: Vendome, 1985.

Kendall, Richard, ed. *Monet by Himself: Paintings, Drawings, Pastels, Letters*. Boston: Little, Brown, 1990.

Levine, Steven Z. *Monet and His Critics*. New York: Garland, 1976.

Pissarro, Joachim. *Monet's Cathedral: Rouen 1892–1894*. New York: Alfred A. Knopf, 1990.

Rewald, John, and Frances Weitzenhoffer, eds. *Aspects of Monet: A Symposium on the Artist's Life and Times*. New York: Harry N. Abrams, 1984.

Seiberling, Grace. *Monet's Series*. New York: Garland, 1981.

Seitz, William C. *Claude Monet*. New York: Harry N. Abrams, 1960.

Spate, Virginia. *Claude Monet: Life and Work*. New York: Rizzoli, 1992.

Stuckey, Charles, ed. *Monet: A Retrospective*. New York: Hugh Lauter Levin, 1985.

Tucker, Paul Hayes. *Monet in the '90s: The Series Paintings*. Boston and New Haven: Museum of Fine Arts Boston in association with Yale University Press, 1989.

First published in 1994 in the United States of America by Rizzoli International Publications, Inc.
300 Park Avenue South
New York, New York 10010

Library of Congress Cataloging-in-Publication Data

Levine, Steven Z.
    Claude Monet / by Steven Z. Levine.
        p.   cm. — (Rizzoli art series)
    Includes bibliographical references.
    ISBN 0-8478-1785-7
    1. Monet, Claude, 1840–1926—Criticism and interpretation.
2. Impressionism (Art)—France. I. Title. II. Series.
ND553.M7L47 1994
759.4—dc20   94-14642
                                                    CIP

Designed by Brian Sisco
Series Editor: Norma Broude
Editor: Charles Miers
Assistant Editor: Cathryn Drake
Compositor: Rose Scarpetis

Front cover: see colorplate 12

Printed in Italy

Index to Colorplates

1. *Landscape at Rouelles*. 1858. This first cataloged painting of Monet's career depicts a solitary male observer seated above a river's reflections, but soon this position within the space of narrative representation in Monet's painting will be appropriated by the artist-spectator, whose self-reflective presence in front of the canvas comes to be implicitly mirrored in the image-generating features of the reflective landscape.

2. *On the Seine at Bennecourt*. 1868. Not only does this painting recall Monet's rivalries with Courbet and Manet in the fringe of foliage and beached boat taken from *Young Ladies on the Banks of the Seine in Summer* (1857) and *The Luncheon on the Grass* (1863), respectively, but it also anticipates Monet's later preoccupation with the mobile screen of inverted reflections as seen by a pair of unseen eyes.

3. *Impression, Sunrise*. 1872. "Wall paper in an embryonic state is still more done than this marine," wrote one critic sarcastically at the time of the first Impressionist exhibition in 1874. Repudiating this oft-repeated charge of sketchy indistinctness, Monet reportedly retorted to his friend Renoir, "Poor blind idiots. They want to see everything clearly, even through the fog."

4. *The Studio-Boat*. 1874. Unexhibited during Monet's lifetime, this painting of his tethered boat and its transient reflection can stand as a "real-allegory" of a mode of naturalistic representation that is at the same time symbolic of the temporal processes, spatial projections, and cultural meanings of self-reflection.

5. *The Pond at Montgeron*. 1876. The identification of the painter's gaze with that of his water-gazing female companion recurs here (plates 2, 7). Part of a never-installed, four-panel decoration at the Hoschedé country estate, this canvas will find its scale and shape repeated in the *Water Lilies* (plates 11, 14).

6. *Fishermen on the Seine at Poissy*. 1882. Two years after the death of his wife, Monet and his two sons and Alice Hoschedé and her six children briefly set up housekeeping at Poissy. Monet made a similar, smaller painting of two fishermen on the Seine viewed from above and reproduced a drawing of this Japanese-inspired work in the journal *L'Art Moderne*.

7. *In the Norwegian Canoe*. c. 1887. Here three of Mme Hoschedé's four daughters double Monet's role of water-gazer in a composition that recollects the mirrored effects of plate 4 even as it quadruples the size of that painting. In scale and subject *The Canoe* recapitulates Monet's *Women in the Garden*, rejected at the Salon of 1867, and anticipates the paintings of the pond at Giverny (plate 13).

8. *The Four Trees*. 1891. Monet exhibited fifteen paintings in his series of *Poplars*, all of them upright except for a horizontal composition that focuses on the sweep of the trees along the bank. In this unique square painting Monet divides his four-trunk field into the sort of rigorous grid that will later resonate throughout much of twentieth-century art.

9. *Rouen Cathedral, West Facade, Sunlight*. 1894. In 1895 Georges Clemenceau, future premier of France, urged the state to acquire Monet's twenty-part series of *Cathedrals* in order to maintain it as a coherent decorative ensemble. In gratitude for the article, Monet proposed to reinstall the exhibition according to the consecutive sequence of gray, white, iridescent, and blue luminosities envisioned by Clemenceau.

10. *The Seine at Giverny*. 1897. The reflective capacities of water transform objects into images; the Impressionist painter deliberately does the same, yet in this "double ornamental cutout" the distinction between reflections and things is elided in a uniformity of surface that mimes the texture of consciousness and could virtually withstand being turned upside down.

11. *Water Lilies*. 1903. One of forty-eight paintings exhibited in 1909 and subsequently sold as but one part of the dismembered whole, this view positions us along the banks of Monet's pond, the hanging fringe of the willow's foliage above our heads and the flowering surface of the water at our feet. The palpable surface at our fingertips vies with the receding space beyond our grasp.

12. *Houses of Parliament, Sunset*. 1904. Like *Impression, Sunrise* of thirty years earlier (plate 3), this painting exploits the natural phenomena of sun, water, and fog in order to transform an observed experience into a dreamlike scene. Is this an evasion of the grimy reality of industrialized London or an affirmation that even there art can safeguard a private sphere of self-reflection?

13. *Corner of the Pond at Giverny*. 1917. In the wartime aftermath of the deaths of his second wife and his elder son, Monet persevered in solitary labor in his garden. Always with him was Blanche Hoschedé-Monet, his wife's daughter and his son's widow, as well as many visitors, so his posture of anxious self-absorption was widely received as an exemplary social act.

14. *Water Lilies: The Irises*. 1916–1923. During the war Monet conceived the idea of a monumental gift of paintings in memorial to the dead. Who are entombed in the Orangerie in Paris where his testamentary gift is housed? Narcissus, Echo, his mother, his wives, his dreams to grasp the bigendered ideal that always eluded his reach. . . .

15. *Self-Portrait*. 1917. Given by Monet to Clemenceau and by the latter to the Louvre after Monet's death, this self-representation of the octogenarian painter is the only one to survive the bouts of mutilation in which its mates perished. Even here Monet portrays himself not as enduring embodiment but as evanescent shade.

1. *Landscape at Rouelles*. 1858. Oil on canvas, 18 x 25¼".
Private collection, Japan. Photograph courtesy Noortman (London) Ltd.

2. On the Seine at Bennecourt, 1868. Oil on canvas, 32 x 39⅝".
The Art Institute of Chicago. Mr. and Mrs. Potter Palmer Collection (1922.427)

3. *Impression, Sunrise*. 1872. Oil on canvas, 18¾ x 24½".
Musée Marmottan, Paris. Photograph courtesy Giraudon/Art Resource, New York

4. *The Studio-Boat.* 1874. Oil on canvas, 19⅝ x 25½".
Rijksmuseum Kröller-Müller, Otterlo, The Netherlands

5. *The Pond at Montgeron*, 1876. Oil on canvas, 67 x 75¼".
Hermitage Museum. St. Petersburg. Photograph courtesy Scala/Art Resource. New York

6. *Fishermen on the Seine at Poissy,* 1882. Oil on canvas, 23⅝ x 31⅞".
Österreichische Galerie, Vienna (no. 1288)

7. *In the Norwegian Canoe*, c. 1887. Oil on canvas, 38⅛ x 51".
Musée d'Orsay, Paris. Photograph courtesy Réunion des Musées Nationaux

8. *The Four Trees.* 1891. Oil on canvas, 32¼ x 32⅛".
The Metropolitan Museum of Art, New York. Bequest of Mrs. H. O. Havemeyer, 1929.
The H. O. Havemeyer Collection (29.100.110)

9. Rouen Cathedral, West Facade, Sunlight. 1894. Oil on canvas, 39½ x 26".
National Gallery of Art, Washington, D.C. Chester Dale Collection

10. *The Seine at Giverny*, 1897. Oil on canvas, 32⅛ x 39⅝".
National Gallery of Art, Washington, D.C. Chester Dale Collection

11. *Water Lilies*. 1903. Oil on canvas. 32 x 40".
The Dayton Art Institute. Gift of Mr. Joseph Rubin

12. *Houses of Parliament, Sunset.* 1904. Oil on canvas, 31½ x 36".
Kaiser Wilhelm Museum, Krefeld, Germany

13. *Corner of the Pond at Giverny.* 1917. Oil on canvas, 46 x 32⅝".
Musée des Beaux-Arts, Grenoble, France. Photograph courtesy Scala/Art Resource, New York

14. *Water Lilies: The Irises*. 1916–1923. Oil on canvas, 78¾ x 236¼".
Kunsthaus Zürich

15. *Self-Portrait.* 1917. Oil on canvas, 27½ x 21⅝".
Musée d'Orsay, Paris. Photograph courtesy Réunion des Musée Nationaux